This Notebook Belongs To

____

Made in the USA
Monee, IL
25 June 2021

72318127R10069